The Cat[a]
OUTLAWS
ON THE LOOSE

Written by
Kate Scott

Etruscan Primary School
Dundee Road
Etruria
Stoke on Trent
ST1 4BS

Illustrated by
Tom Bonson

Published by Pearson Education Limited, Edinburgh Gate, Harlow, Essex, CM20 2JE.

www.pearsonschools.co.uk

Text © Kate Scott 2013

Designed by Jo Samways
Original illustrations © Pearson Education Limited 2013
Illustrated by Tom Bonson, Advocate
Cover design by Tom Bonson and Jo Samways

The right of Kate Scott to be identified as author of this work has been asserted by her in accordance with the Copyright, Designs and Patents Act 1988.

First published 2013

17 16 15 14 13
10 9 8 7 6 5 4 3 2 1

British Library Cataloguing in Publication Data
A catalogue record for this book is available from the British Library

ISBN 978 0 435 14370 1

Copyright notice
All rights reserved. No part of this publication may be reproduced in any form or by any means (including photocopying or storing it in any medium by electronic means and whether or not transiently or incidentally to some other use of this publication) without the written permission of the copyright owner, except in accordance with the provisions of the Copyright, Designs and Patents Act 1988 or under the terms of a licence issued by the Copyright Licensing Agency, Saffron House, 6–10 Kirby Street, London EC1N 8TS (www.cla.co.uk) . Applications for the copyright owner's written permission should be addressed to the publisher.

Printed and bound in the UK by Ashford Colour Press.

Acknowledgements
We would like to thank Bangor Central Integrated Primary School, Northern Ireland; Bishop Henderson Church of England Primary School, Somerset; Bletchingdon Parochial Church of England Primary School, Oxfordshire; Brookside Community Primary School, Somerset; Bude Park Primary School, Hull; Carisbrooke Church of England Primary School, Isle of Wight; Cheddington Combined School, Buckinghamshire; Dair House Independent School, Buckinghamshire; Glebe Infant School, Gloucestershire; Henley Green Primary School, Coventry; Lovelace Primary School, Surrey; Our Lady of Peace Junior School, Slough; Tackley Church of England Primary School, Oxfordshire; and Twyford Church of England School, Buckinghamshire for their invaluable help in the development and trialling of the Bug Club resources.

Every effort has been made to contact copyright holders of material reproduced in this book. Any omissions will be rectified in subsequent printings if notice is given to the publishers.

CONTENTS

Chapter One	5
Chapter Two	14
Chapter Three	25
Chapter Four	35
Chapter Five	50

CHAPTER ONE

Tess took a pitchfork to another ball of tumbleweed and tossed it out of the yard. She turned at the sound of a whooped "Hoo boy!" followed by a loud thump.

Jim was flat on his back in the middle of the yard, surrounded by the four large sacks of flour he had been carrying. The chicken Jim had tripped over ran, squawking, into the safety of the hen-house.

"Are you all right?" Tess couldn't help smiling. Her brother was always falling over. He had to be the clumsiest boy in the West.

"I'm fine." Jim got up and brushed his breeches down. He never seemed bothered by his accidents. He picked up the sacks of flour and slung them back over his shoulder.

He grinned over at Tess. "Ma told me I can put in some catapult practice after I pile these up."

Tess decided she'd better put the chickens away before he started practising. Maybe the horse and Stub the mule too. Jim had a habit of hitting a lot of livestock when he was practising with his catapult. She'd got smacked by a catapult pellet more than once herself. It was just as well she was going to be lending Ma a hand in the kitchen, after her outdoor chores were done. It would be safer.

The sound of an approaching horse made Tess and Jim stop what they were doing. Mr James, their neighbour from the ranch ten miles up the track, came cantering up.

"Hello, kids." Mr James tipped his hat to Tess, but didn't get off his horse. "I came to warn you all not to be going into Lizard's Lick for a while."

"Not go into Lizard's Lick? Why?" Lizard's Lick was the nearest town to the ranch. Tess stared up at Mr James.

His usual smile had been replaced by a deeply serious frown.

"Butch Cassidy and his gang robbed the town bank last night. Cleaned the safe right out – they say it had more than five hundred dollars in it," Mr James told them, shaking his head. "The gang tied up the Deputy when he tried to stop them riding off. The Sheriff thinks they're still in the area, hoping to come back and do some more robbing before they move on. He wants to catch them, but they're a dangerous bunch all right."

"Butch Cassidy!" Jim's eyes were shining. "He's the most famous robber in the West!"

"That's nothing for him to be proud of," Mr James told Jim sternly. "He's meaner than a snake, remember that."

"Yes, sir," Jim said, adopting a solemn face.

"Now you make sure to tell your Ma and Pa. And don't you be going far while those outlaws are on the loose. I've got to keep riding on and make sure the other ranchers know."

"Yes, sir," Tess and Jim said together.

As soon as Mr James was out of sight, Jim turned to his sister. "I'll fix them, Tess! With Annie Oakley's catapult I can do anything! I'm going to go after those outlaws and bring them into the Sheriff!"

"You're crazier than a racoon!" Tess stabbed her pitchfork into the ground. "Jim, there's absolutely no way you're going after those outlaws!"

"You know how good my catapulting is," Jim replied. "Remember the show with Annie Oakley and Buffalo Bill?"

Tess did remember. Her brother had put on an amazing performance – completely by accident. He hadn't hit a single thing he'd been aiming at. She didn't think he'd ever hit anything he'd been aiming at. Her brother was brave and he meant well, but as a rider and a shooter? He was about as much use as a fork with a bowl of hot soup.

"Remember, Annie said I was her hero!" Jim continued, his eyes shining. "I'll have them rounded up in no time! I could do with a faster ride than Stub, but I guess Pa wouldn't let me go on his horse ..."

For a moment Tess couldn't speak. Her brother had always been a daydreamer but this was a step too far.

"Jim, you can't go after the outlaws. You heard what Mr James just said. They're dangerous."

Jim grinned. "Don't worry, Sis, I have a plan."

Tess crossed her arms. "What kind of a plan?"

"I'll sneak up on them late at night and catapult the ground around their horses to scare them away. Then I'll tie the gang up while they're sleeping and drag them back to the Sheriff's office in town."

Tess stared. "And you're going to do this by yourself?"

Jim nodded. "Sure thing. I'll be back by morning."

Clearly, her brother had taken leave of his senses, but Tess knew one thing – she couldn't let Jim go after Butch Cassidy and his gang. She had to do whatever it took to stop him.

Chapter Two

If Jim was busy then he couldn't leave, Tess decided. So she'd just have to keep him busy.

Tess put her hand to her head and groaned. "Oooowwwww."
Jim was shovelling the yard and didn't hear. Tess groaned again.

"ARRRRGHHHHHH!"

Jim stopped shovelling and looked over. "Are you okay, Sis?"

Tess shook her head. "Ooooooooooh." She sat down on one of the logs Pa had chopped earlier that morning and winced as if any movement hurt her.

Jim came over, his forehead creased with concern. "What's the matter?"

"I'm not feeling so well, Jim," Tess told him. "I'm feeling really bad."

"Is it your head? Shall I fetch the Doc?"

Tess felt a flush of guilt about lying to her brother, but it was for his own good.

"No, don't fetch the Doc. I'll be okay. I've just come over all achy." Tess smiled weakly. "But, Jim – do you think you could do my chores for me? Ma gave me some extra ones too and I don't think I can manage it all ..."

Jim frowned. "I kind of wanted to get on the road to get after the gang."

"Please, Jim? I don't feel good – and if Ma ends up hollering at me, I'm going to feel even worse."

Tess slumped her shoulders and let out another low moan. She had to make Jim fall for her act.

Jim patted Tess's shoulder. "Sure, Sis, of course I'll help. You take it easy."

Tess smiled. "Okay, here's the list." She started counting off on her fingers. "Milk the cows, feed the chickens, collect the eggs, muck out the stables, sweep the yard, clean the tack, bring in the water, scrub the potatoes, collect the kindling and make up the fire.

Then polish the windows, hang out the clothes and beat the rugs."

Jim whistled. "I'd better get going, if I'm going to do all that and my own work too."

"Thanks, Jim," Tess said. It was too bad she had to give her brother so much to do – but she had to stop him from doing something so crazy.

Jim smiled at her. "You just make sure you feel better. Why don't you go lie down in the stables for a while?"

Tess nodded and stood up slowly, as if it was hard for her to move. She limped towards the stables.

"Hey, Sis, you hurt your leg too?"

Tess turned around. Jim was looking very puzzled. Maybe the limp had been too much.

"Just knocked it on the wood pile," she said and went off walking normally.

Tess sat down on one of the hay bales in the stables and listened to her brother working outside. Every so often there was a thump as he tripped or knocked something over. She winced when she heard the clang of the metal milking bucket. If Jim spilt the milk for the morning, Ma would be madder than a rattlesnake without a tail. It couldn't be helped though.

A little while later she heard Jim whistling to his dog, Bullseye, while he rounded up the horses into the corral.

Jim could get Bullseye to do anything – except stay close when Jim had his catapult out.

But even with all that Tess had given him to do, it was only an couple of hours or so later when Jim poked his head round the stable door. "All done, Tess," he told her. "I'm going to saddle up Stub and get after the gang."

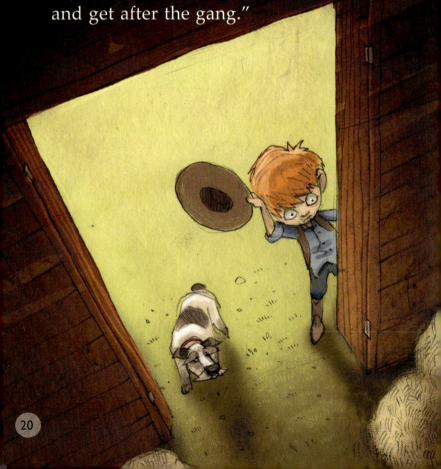

"No! Wait!" Tess said, standing up quickly. "I ... I forgot that Pa wanted you to chop some wood today."

"But he just chopped a bunch early this morning," Jim said. "Are you sure he wanted me to chop more?"

Tess nodded. "Yes, a lot more he said. As much as you can."

Jim sighed. "Okay, if you say so, Sis. I guess I'd better do it."

Tess watched him as he went out of the stables again. Maybe chopping wood after all the other chores would tire him out. He'd think twice about going after the gang if he was so exhausted he could hardly ride – wouldn't he?

But an hour later, Jim was back. He might be clumsy, but he was a quick worker. Too quick, Tess thought. He was making it too hard to keep him safe.

"You're done already?" she asked.

"Yup," Jim said triumphantly. "I've chopped all there was. And now I'm going," he added firmly. "I've told Ma I'm going camping down by the creek and I've packed my saddle bags. I'm going to catch that Butch and his gang and make sure they don't do any more harm in Lizard's Lick." He held up the catapult that Annie Oakley had given him. "I'd like to see them outshoot me with this."

Tess thought they could probably outshoot her brother with anything, but she decided not to say so. Ever since Annie Oakley had given Jim her catapult, her brother had been convinced that he was a proper sharp shooter.

"You should leave capturing the gang to the Sheriff, Jim," Tess said. "That's his job." She caught the cuff of his sleeve and repeated, "You heard what Mr James said – they're dangerous."

"Don't worry," Jim smiled. "I'll be fine. I've been practising, and I have a plan."

Tess groaned as Jim left, whistling to Bullseye to follow. Her plan hadn't worked at all.

She was going to have to do something drastic.

Chapter Three

Tess went outside as Jim saddled up his mule, Stub, and swung up on his back. He waved at Tess. "I'll be back before you know it, Sis," he told her. Then he turned and rode out of the ranch and down the track towards Lizard's Lick with Bullseye following along behind.

"You'll be back all right," Tess said under her breath. "I'm going to make sure of it."

Tess went in the house and told Ma that she'd decided to join Jim on his camping trip.

She packed some supplies and picked up an old blanket to sling over her saddle. Then she headed back into the stables, towards the wooden box where Pa kept some of his old work clothes. She had it all figured out. She was going to disguise herself as one of Butch Cassidy's followers and lead Jim as far away as possible from the real gang.

Ten minutes later, Tess was ready. She had put on her Pa's dirtiest working coat, which came down to her ankles, and an enormous hat he only ever wore around the ranch because of the big holes it had in the brim. She'd rubbed dirt all over her face and drawn on a moustache and stubble with a piece of charcoal. She looked at herself in the water barrel in the yard. Not totally convincing, she thought, but from several feet away she thought she might pass as a mean gang member.

She just couldn't let Jim get close enough to guess who she really was …

Tess saddled up one of the new, young ponies Pa had recently bought, figuring that Jim was less likely to recognise it. She set off along one of the trails that led away from the ranch through the woods.

She was going to have to get ahead of Jim and then stay ahead if she was going to convince him she wasn't anyone he knew. Luckily, Jim's mule Stub was one of the slowest four-legged creatures in the West. And Jim was one of the worst riders. She would soon catch up.

Tess pulled her hat down low and then urged her pony to a gallop. She thundered along the path, brushing hanging branches away from her face as they swung into her way.

As Tess reached the edge of the woods, she turned and headed towards the track Jim had taken. She needed to appear up ahead of him. She glanced back to see if she could see him. She'd timed it just right – he was about half a mile behind her. But what was he doing? He'd wandered completely off the path and wasn't even looking at the track ahead. "Whoa, boy," she told the pony and reigned him in.

She kept her eyes on Jim as he got off Stub and started to hunt about in the grass next to the track.

What's he doing? Tess thought. Then she saw Bullseye's tail wagging in the long grass. *Jim must think Bullseye was on to the gang's trail,* she thought to herself. But she could see from the way Bullseye was zigzagging from side to side that whatever Bullseye was tracking, it wasn't human – unless that human had a lot of trouble walking straight.

Tess grinned. Maybe Bullseye was going to do her job for her. She tied her pony to a tree just off the path and settled down in the long grass to wait. From where she was, she could see that Bullseye was looping round in circles. At this rate, Jim wouldn't get anywhere near the gang!

Tess watched for an hour as Bullseye ran back and forth, with Jim close behind.

Finally, Bullseye pounced. Jim leapt after him and grabbed. Tess laughed as she saw him hold up …

… a cute, furry prairie dog. It squeaked in panic as Jim dropped it with disgust and then whistled at Bullseye to stop him chasing it.

Tess scrambled to her feet. Now the fun was over. Jim was getting back on the track, and it was time to put her plan into action.

Staying low to the ground, Tess ran back to where she had tethered her pony and quickly mounted it. Then she got back on the trail, glancing behind her to check where Jim was. She didn't want to put so much distance between them that Jim would lose her. It was time to act the part of a mean gang member ...

Tess pulled out her catapult and a tin can she'd tucked in Pa's overcoat. She threw the can high into the air and then took careful aim with her catapult. The pellet hit the can with a great smack. At the same time, she lowered her voice to a growl and yelled out. "WAIT UP THERE, BUTCH. I'M GOING TO CATCH YOU UP!"

She craned her neck and snuck a look behind her. Jim had heard her all right. He was clearly jabbing Stub with his boots, trying to get him to go as fast as he could – which wasn't very fast.

Tess smiled to herself. She'd done it. She'd caught her brother like a fish on a pole. Now all she had to do was lead him as far away from Lizard's Lick as she could, so that there was no chance of him running into the real Butch.

Chapter Four

Tess rode through the afternoon, the sun beating down on top of her hat. Tumbleweeds rolled across her path and hawks swooped overhead. She took sips of water from her flask and snacked on bread that Ma had given her. She was getting tired, but it was good to know her plan was working. As the sun started to go down, Tess began to relax. Jim was still half a mile behind her and they were now far enough away from Lizard's Lick that she figured they were safe.

The gang must be camping near to the town if they were planning another raid.

As the temperature began to drop, Tess shivered. Maybe she should set up camp. Jim wouldn't carry out his plan with her on her own. He'd be waiting until she led him to the gang – which of course she wasn't going to do.

She rode her pony on, sidestepping the great balls of tumbleweed, heading for the tall trees in the distance that stretched towards the evening sky. The sun was low on the horizon. It would be dark soon. Tess slowed, glancing back at Jim. It looked like Stub was getting tired; he was moving so slowly, and Jim was almost swaying on his back. He was probably tuckered out after all those chores today. It was time to stop.

Up ahead, Tess spotted what looked like a deserted shack. She decided to make for it to get some rest.

When she was about ten feet away from the shack, Tess got off her pony and approached it on foot, just to be safe. A moment later, she froze at the sound of voices inside. She looked over her shoulder. Jim had clearly decided the mysterious stranger had stopped for the night and was now letting Stub graze nearby. Tess dropped to her belly and wiggled forward to try and hear who was in the shack. She came up close and saw that there was a small hole in the wall. As quietly as she could, she pressed her eye up close to it.

Inside, there were several men sitting on the dirty wooden floor. The largest and meanest looking of the lot was counting up a huge stack of dollar bills. The men wore dark clothes and two of them had thick dark stubble on their chins.

"Seems to me we should just move on to the next town," said one. He kept looking nervously over at the door.

"You chickening out, Gus?" A bigger man with fair hair laughed. He held up a fistful of dollars. "Haven't got stomach enough to go back for the rest of what Lizard's Lick got for us?"

"You come over here and call me chicken to my face, Shane!" Gus said. "I'll show you who's a chicken!"

"Pipe down you two," snarled the man who had been bent over the money. He got to his feet. He looked taller and stronger – and meaner – than all of the others. "We're not leaving Lizard's Lick until we've got what we came for – all of the cash. Understood?"

There was a chorus of agreement from the other men.

"Yeah, Butch."

"Okay, Butch."

Tess felt a shudder run through her body. She hadn't led Jim away from the gang – she'd led him right to them! This was a disaster!

"Now look," Butch said. "This is what we're going to do." His boots clunked as he moved around the shack. "We're going to wait 'til it's totally dark and then we're going to ride into town and get ourselves that money from the store.

You can bet your boots that they've got a pile of dollars hidden out back. We just need to go and get it."

"You make it sound easy, Butch," Shane said.

"It is easy, straw for brains," said Gus.

"CUT OUT THAT ARGUING YOU TWO!" Butch shouted.

Shane and Gus fell silent and the others kept quiet.

"Once we've got the money, we'll get out of here and move on further West. Lizard's Lick won't be worth a lick." Butch paused while the men laughed nastily. Tess tightened her fists. How dare he say that about her home town!

"So get your stuff together and we'll show that Sheriff that he's as much use to his town as a catapult is to a baby."

They laughed again. Tess was so mad she could spit! Now she understood why Jim had come out here. He was right. They had to get rid of this gang – and fast. But she also had to make sure Jim didn't realise they were here. His idea of how to get rid of them and hers just didn't match up.

Tess stood up slowly to avoid making any noise. She had to get back to Lizard's Lick and warn the Sheriff, but first she had to get Jim away from here and make sure he followed her and not the gang.

She was going to have to move quickly. Tess walked backwards so that she could keep an eye on the shack. She could still hear the men's voices, but she could no longer hear what they were saying. Now she was aware of every sound – the crunch of her boots on the ground, the snuffling of her pony behind her. It was nearly dark, but she could just make out the shape of Stub and Jim in the distance. At least she knew they weren't far away.

She patted her pony as she came up to him. "Shush, fella," she told him. "We've got to keep real quiet now."

The pony snuffled again as Tess put her foot in the stirrup and swung herself into the saddle. Now it was time for the tricky bit. She had to pass Jim close enough so that he saw her, but not so close that he recognised her.

"Come on," she whispered to her pony. "Let's go snare my brother again."

She began to ride back the way they had come, directly towards Stub, who was now standing next to a clump of gorse, dipping his head to munch on the grass. She'd gone a few feet more when she heard snoring – Jim had fallen asleep while still sitting on Stub! She guessed those chores earlier had tired him out after all …

"Sorry, brother – no time for napping now," Tess whispered to herself.

She guided her pony to the right of Stub and then gave a deep cough as she rode past her brother.

Jim sprang up straight, jerking Stub's reins. "What is it, fella?" Down on the ground, Bullseye barked.

Tess cringed, looking back over her shoulder at the shack. The gang were surely far enough away not to have heard, weren't they?

She urged the pony on a few steps and put her hand up to her hat to yank it down over her face.

Behind her, she heard Jim patting Stub and whispering to Bullseye. It was time to get moving. She had to lead Jim in to Lizard's Lick and find the Sheriff before the gang got to the store. She gave another short cough and started to ride.

As she trotted along at a pace that she knew Jim could keep up with, Tess didn't see the outline of a group of men on horses, watching her silhouette as it moved through the night. She didn't see how one by one, they started to follow after her …

Chapter Five

As Tess rode the track leading to Lizard's Lick, the moon came out from behind the clouds. Now the way ahead was coloured silver and each bush and tree cast a shadow. Tess wanted to go faster to make sure she reached the Sheriff in time, but she couldn't afford to lose Jim, so she kept the pace steady and crossed her fingers on the reins.

She tried not to look behind her too often, in case Jim caught sight of her face in the bright moonlight. However, as she drew closer to town, she risked one quick glance behind her to make sure he was still following.

She had been going too slowly after all. Jim was right behind her – and up on the horizon, so were Butch and his gang!

Tess let out a gasp. This was worse than running into a pit full of snakes!

She realised she couldn't get away in time – her secret was out. In seconds, Jim was close enough to see her by the light of the moon.

His mouth gaped in shock. "Sis! What are you doing here? And what's all over your face?"

"There's no time to explain," Tess said. "Butch Cassidy's gang are after us, look!"

Jim whipped round and saw the gang approaching on the horizon.

"They're still a way away – if we hurry, we can get to the Sheriff and warn him," Tess said.

Jim shook his head. "No way! We've got to stand up to them, Sis."

Tess clapped her hand to her hat, exasperated. "Jim! There's a whole gang coming! And there's just me and you!" she exclaimed.

Jim smiled. "And Annie Oakley's catapult – and Bullseye."

Tess stared at him. This wasn't going to work. She knew her brother well enough to know that when he got an idea stuck in his head, it stayed stuck, and they were losing time arguing about it.

"Fine," she said. "But we start out hiding behind those trees over there."

Jim opened his mouth to protest, but Tess held up her hand. "If we're doing this, we're doing it my way, okay? It means we can surprise them ... "

... or change our minds when you see how many there are of them, and how mean they are, Tess said to herself.

Jim grinned. "Okay, Sis, let's get out the way – ready to spring out at 'em!"

"Let's just get hidden first," Tess said.

They rode over to the small group of hickory trees that were a little way down the trail and pulled up behind them. They peeked out between the branches, as the gang of riders got closer and closer. Soon they could hear the thunder of the horse's hooves.

Tess's heart began to pound in her chest and she felt her hands go clammy. She snuck a look at Jim, hoping that seeing what was coming was making him see sense. If they stayed put, maybe the gang would just ride on past them.

But Jim was still smiling. "Don't you worry, Sis, it's going to be fine."

Tess couldn't help smiling back. Her brother might be the clumsiest boy in the West but he was also the bravest, and the most fiercely protective.

As the gang drew near to their hiding spot, Tess held her breath.

Then Jim suddenly gave a piercing whistle. Immediately, Bullseye ran out in front of the first set of riders and began to bark furiously, running in small tight circles. The horses at the front started to rear up and some the gang started to shout.

"It's an ambush, Butch!"

"Watch out! There's a mad dog!"

Tess watched in shock and horror as Jim jabbed at Stub's sides. "Come on, boy, let's go!" he shouted.

But Stub was clearly sick and tired of riding. He was exhausted after having ridden all day and enough was enough. He took Jim out onto the track but emerged from behind the trees bucking and kicking like a wild pony, determined to get Jim off of his back.

"Whoooooo!" shouted Jim as he clung on to Stub's back. Stub tore up and down, going faster than Tess had ever see him go. In the moonlight he looked bigger than he was, casting long dark shadows on the ground as he reared up.

Tess looked on, frozen to the spot, until she realised she was going to have to help. She loaded her catapult and aimed it up high into the hickory tree they were standing under.

A moment later she fired and brought down a torrent of hickory nuts on the gang's heads.

There were shouts of "Ow!" and "Quick! Watch your back!" and "We're under attack!"

Jim charged round on Stub, trying to get him to chase the others, but he was only managing to enrage his mule even more. Stub was bucking so furiously that it was a miracle Jim was still in the saddle.

"Hoooo boy!" Jim kept on yelling as Stub jerked and bucked. Tess could see that to the gang members, it seemed as if there were dozens of them.

Now the rest of the horses were trying to escape the chaos. One of the bandit's horses tore away into the prairies, whinnying as he went, his rider out of control.

Tess brought down another load of nuts to the ground so that they popped like popcorn. Then she put her hands to her mouth and gave a loud "Whoop!" that echoed around the prairie.

She quickly rode to another part of the trees and shouted out in her lowest voice, "I'm on my way, boss!" before firing down another load of nuts onto the gang.

Bullseye was still barking madly as he ran about from one side of the trail to the other, and then back again. He leapt up at one of the riders and growled as he hung on the gang member's boot.

"Hey, get off me, mutt!" The man tried to shake Bullseye off as Bullseye chewed furiously on his toe.

"We got to get out of here, boss!" another member of the gang cried out. "This gang's bigger than us by far!"

Butch, who was trying to control his own horse, gave a brief nod. "All right, let's go. I hate this stupid town anyway," he snarled. "Let's get moving!" Butch waved the command and turned his

horse around. The gang started riding out into the prairie, away from Lizard's Lick. Soon the thundering hooves were nothing but a noise in the distance.

Tess came out from behind the trees. Where was Jim? "Jim? Where are you?" she called out.

"Over here, Sis!"

Tess ran over to a bush by the side of the trail and found Jim lying flat on his back. "Are you okay?"

Jim grinned and sat up. "Sure, I'm okay. Did you see my riding, Sis? It was amazing! I managed to scare them all off and I didn't even have to use Annie Oakley's catapult!"

Tess gave him her hand to help him up to his feet. She grinned back. "Yeah, you were amazing, Jim."

Jim nodded, satisfied. "When Annie Oakley comes back to Lizard's Lick, we're sure going to have a lot to tell her, aren't we?"

"We sure are," Tess told him. "But for now – please can we just go home?"

Find it!

How did Tess and Jim see off Butch Cassidy and his gang?

Share it!

Wanted!

Re-read the story making notes on the descriptions of Butch Cassidy and his gang. When you've finished, write a comic strip about the robbers and their life of crime.

Think about who will catch the gang in the end, and how? Will it be someone from the Pinkerton Detective Agency? Decide what characters to use; then plan your story. Draw panels and use comic strip words like 'Bang!' and 'Arghhhh!' to bring your story to life. When you've finished, give your comic strip to a friend to read.

Want to know more?

Find out more about the period of American history called the Wild West. You could watch cowboy films online to learn what life was really like on the ranch!

THE CATAPULT KID
OUTLAWS ON THE LOOSE

**Red B
NC 5B**

Annie Oakley called Jim her 'hero' and now he thinks he can do anything ... even catch Butch Cassidy and his mean gang of crooks! His sister Tess is less sure and comes up with a plan to stop him. Can she keep him away from the outlaws, or will she run into a whole lot of trouble?

"I think Jim is very brave!" Tilly

www.bugclub.co.uk

www.pearsonschools.co.uk
myorders@pearson.com
T 0845 630 33 33
F 0845 630 77 77

ISBN 978-0-435-14370

ALWAYS LEARNING

PEARSON